THE WORLD AROUND ME

ANIMALS

IN MY WORLD

Written by

Hermione Redshaw

KidHaven
PUBLISHING

Published in 2023 by **KidHaven Publishing,
an Imprint of Greenhaven Publishing, LLC**
2544 Clinton St., Buffalo, NY 14224

© 2022 Booklife Publishing
This edition is published by arrangement with
Booklife Publishing

Written by: Hermione Redshaw
Edited by: William Anthony
Illustrated by: Amy Li

Font (cover, page 1) courtesy of cuppuccino on
Shutterstock.com. With thanks to Getty Images,
Thinkstock Photo, and iStockphoto.

Cataloging-in-Publication Data

Names: Redshaw, Hermione, author. I Li, Amy,
illustrator.
Title: Animals in my world / by Hermione Redshaw,
illustrated by Amy Li.
Description: New York : KidHaven Publishing, 2023.
I Series: The world around me
Identifiers: ISBN 9781534543225 (pbk.) I
ISBN 9781534543249 (library bound) I
ISBN 9781534543256 (ebook)
Subjects: LCSH: Animals--Juvenile literature.
Classification: LCC QL49.R394 2023 I
DDC 590--dc23

Manufactured in the United States of America

CPSIA compliance information: Batch #CWKH23
For further information contact Greenhaven Publishing LLC
at 1-844-317-7404.

Please visit our website, www.greenhavenpublishing.com.
For a free color catalog of all our high-quality books,
call toll free 1-844-317-7404 or fax 1-844-317-7405.

Find us on

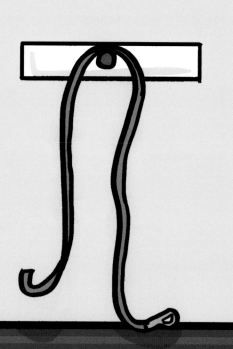

Lizzie knows all about animals!
She loves every kind of animal.

Lizzie walks her **dog.**

Dogs have fur.

Dogs can be **big** or small.

Lizzie's dog wags her tail.
Lizzie knows she is happy.

Cats have fur.

They lick themselves clean.

Cats meow at Lizzie.
They hiss at birds.

Birds have feathers.

They fly with wings.

Lizzie sees birds everywhere.
Some birds cannot fly.

Lizzie sees sheep at the farm.

Sheep have lots of wool.

Sheep get hot in summer.
The farmer cuts their wool.

Cows eat grass in the fields.

They make milk.

The cows Lizzie sees
are black and white.

Some cows
are brown.

Fish live in water.

They have scales.

Some fish are small.

Other fish can be
REALLY BIG!

15

Lizzie visits giraffes at the zoo.

Giraffes eat leaves from tall trees.

Giraffes are
covered in
brown spots.

Their necks are
very long.

17

Lions are big cats.

Wild lions hunt for food.

Male lions have longer fur
around their heads.

This is called a mane.

Monkeys have fur.

Most monkeys have tails.

Monkeys are good
at swinging
from trees.

21

Snakes have long bodies.
They have no arms or legs.

Snakes slither
on the ground.

They stick their tongues
out and hiss.

Lizzie's favorite animal is a lion!

What is **your** favorite animal?